MW00975624

Great Careers for People Interested in
Travel & Tourism

by
Donna Sharon & Jo Anne Sommers

YOUTH MIDDLE SCHOOL
MEDIA CENTER

An imprint of Gale Research,
An ITP Information/Reference Group Company

Changing the Way the World Learns

NEW YORK • LONDON • BONN • BOSTON • DETROIT • MADRID
MELBOURNE • MEXICO CITY • PARIS • SINGAPORE • TOKYO
TORONTO • WASHINGTON • ALBANY NY • BELMONT CA • CINCINNATI OH

© 1996
Trifolium Books Inc. and Weigl Educational Publishers Limited

First published in Canada by Trifolium Books Inc. and Weigl
Educational Publishers Limited

U•X•L is the exclusive publisher of the U.S. library edition of Series 3.

An imprint of
Gale Research
835 Penobscot Bldg.
Detroit, MI 48226

Library of Congress Catalog Card Number 95-62267
ISBN 0-7876-0862-9

Acknowledgments
The authors and the publishers wish to thank
those people whose careers are featured in this
book for allowing us to interview and
photograph them. Their love for their chosen
careers has made our task an enjoyable one.
The authors would also like to thank the
following people for their assistance with
specific profiles: Bonnie Hector: Anne Marie
Placide, Richard Pinnock (Matrix Marketing);
Lois Wong: Heddy Chase Ratner (Manager of
The Bay), Michelle Rouleau (American Express
Public Relations), Nancy Eskin (American
Express Public Relations), Cathy Ann
LePichouron; John McComber: Sherri
Lockwood (Four Seasons Public Relations).

Design concept: Julian Cleva
Design and layout: Warren Clark
Editors: Susan Lawrence, Rosemary Tanner
Project coordinator, proofreader: Diane Klim
Production coordinator: Amanda Woodrow
Content review: Mary Kay Winter, Julie Czerneda

Printed and bound in Canada
10 9 8 7 6 5 4 3 2 1

This book's text stock contains more than 50% recycled paper.

Contents

Featured profiles

How can you play a big part in a major festival? *Ask*
Bonnie Hector — Festival Organizer   **4**

What did 18th-century soldiers use for toilet paper? *Ask*
Tracy Macdonnell — Historical Interpreter   **10**

How can a meeting planner who's blind assess unfamiliar rooms? *Ask*
**Frances Tanner —
Meeting and Convention Planner**   **16**

How can you reduce gasoline spills in lakes and rivers? *Ask*
**Dawn & Wally Tabobondung —
Marina Operators**   **22**

What are "front-of-the-house" hotel staff? *Ask*
John McComber — Guest Services Manager   **28**

How many time zones are there in Russia? *Ask*
Lois Wong — Travel Agent   **34**

Careers at a glance

Who follows up complaints about an airline meal? *Ask*
Harold Zutz — Airline On-Board Service Manager   **40**

Where do tourists sleep while on safari? *Ask*
Helen Huggett — Safari Planner   **41**

How far ahead of time do newspapers plan travel articles? *Ask*
Catherine George — Travel Writer   **42**

Where are the Galapagos Islands? *Ask*
Bob Khasnabish — Travel Entrepreneur   **43**

Who Got the Job?   **45**

Index/Credits/Answers   **48**

Bonnie Hector

Festival Organizer

PERSONAL PROFILE

Career: Festival organizer. "Every August we produce a large festival showcasing Caribbean culture."

Interests: "I go to lots of musical shows and theater. Whenever I travel I always plan to go to some musical event."

Latest accomplishment: "After the festival is over, we have an Awards Evening. One year, I organized the whole event by myself. I chose the site, arranged for over 400 guests, selected the buffet dinner, and ordered individual trophies for 35 award winners!"

Why I do what I do: "I love it. I enjoy creating the opportunities for the artists to perform."

I am: "Confident, independent, and happy to be working with people."

What I wanted to be when I was in school: "I was good at math and science and I wanted to be a pharmacist. I was on a waiting list for pharmacy school, but then we moved and I started doing other things."

What a festival organizer does

For a really popular public event, you need an attraction that touches and moves people. Championship sports teams, national holidays, or a Santa Claus parade can be the focus for a celebration that gets everyone out enjoying themselves. The culture of the Caribbean provides the heart of the Caribana Festival, held each August in Toronto, Ontario. Festival organizer Bonnie Hector works all year coordinating the massive two-week event. "The main attraction is the parade. Over a million people come to see it every year. There are a lot of other events, many of them organized by volunteers. Some events are free to the public.

"When I first started there were only two of us working part time in a little office down the street. Because we've been attracting more and more people and getting more sponsorship and support, we now have seven full-time staff as well as lots of volunteers working on the festival."

Planning ahead

Festival organizers like Bonnie attend many meetings to discuss, design, and promote the event. They plan the dates and choose locations that will hold all the people they expect will attend. They develop the special features of each event and estimate the budget (the amount of money) needed to produce them. For large events like Caribana, the

Participants often spend months preparing their elaborate costumes.

organizers often hire and supervise contractors to provide publicity, food, souvenirs, and sales staff for the event itself. Organizers also make sure that all the preparations are on schedule.

A variety of tasks

Depending on how many staff are sharing the work, a festival organizer's tasks could include many different jobs. "I coordinate about 200 marketplace vendors who sell food and crafts on the day of the parade." Bonnie also manages more than 200 volunteers who plan and run the other activities. "We hire a public relations company to handle publicity, prepare news releases, and organize media coverage. And some of our staff and volunteers sell tickets and get any necessary permits from the city."

A festival organizer may keep track of finances, collecting money and paying the bills. For the event itself, someone may hire technicians to operate lighting and sound systems, and rent equipment such as tables and chairs, trailers, and barricades for crowd control. "My responsibility," says Bonnie, "is to make sure the festival is ready to go — on time!"

Everyone loves a parade. But it must be organized ahead of time, especially a parade as large as Caribana's.

All in a day's work

There are no daily routines in the work of a festival organizer. As Bonnie says, "Every day, something different happens." Throughout the year, preparations are underway for the next festival. "We have an official festival launch and warm-up party at City Hall, a Junior Carnival, sunset cruises, a competition for King and Queen of the Bands, carnival dances before and after the huge parade, and a music festival."

An important part of Bonnie's job is arranging for about 40 bands to participate in the parade. She is a member of the committee that assesses the applications from the bands. "All the bands portray a unique historic or fantasy topic. Each band must have at least 75 performers. The largest bands also have more than ten costume sections with as many as 1 000 people altogether." With their applications, bands must show their costume designs and describe their portrayals in the parade. "Once the bands are approved, I register the band leaders and collect their entry fees."

Organizing the volunteers

Volunteers produce the masquerade and other

artistic events in the festival, such as the Junior Carnival and the competition for King and Queen of the Festival. "They help make all the plans," notes Bonnie. "About 60 workers are involved in each of the masquerade events. I get to know all of the volunteers and help new people find the best place to get involved."

Some volunteers help to answer the thousands of telephone calls at the Caribana Festival Office. They are trained on the job, working alongside staff. From all over North America, people call at all hours, seven days a week, to find out about the festival. Bonnie has to be sure that the phone volunteers can answer all their questions.

For the parade, two experienced

volunteers are assigned to each of the 40 bands to act as marshals. "They make sure that the crowds are out of the way so that the bands can keep moving. Another dozen volunteers help the police keep the parade flowing smoothly."

Setting up the marketplace

During the early years of the festival, when it was smaller, Bonnie found it easy to organize the marketplace. "I invited the vendors to come early in the day and assigned them their spots as they arrived. But as the festival grew, a lot of vendors came to the site at the same time, and getting them all settled was chaotic," recalls Bonnie. "Now I have a list of all the sites in my office. Vendors

Spirits run high as all the bands compete to be King and Queen of the Bands in an evening event held midway through the festival.

The logo for the Caribbean Cultural Committee, which organizes the Caribana Festival, is always two dancers. Each year, a competition is held to create a new design using the logo. The winning design appears on all the posters, promotional material, souvenirs, caps, and T-shirts.

come in ahead of time and pick their spots. The marketplace has also been redesigned so that all of the vendors are in one row close to the main walkway."

Local businesses and larger companies set up stalls in the marketplace. Most food vendors at Caribana sell Caribbean foods such as curries, rotis, palau, or jerk-spiced chicken. Craft vendors sell T-shirts, paintings, wood carvings, woven baskets, and ceramics, and official souvenirs such as pens, hats, cassettes and CDs, posters, and magazines.

Bonnie also works with Public Health departments to make sure that the vendors are in safe locations and follow the health rules. "I arrange for vendors to attend a training session to ensure that they handle the food safely in their outdoor locations."

Where are the restrooms?

When more than a million people gather to watch a huge parade, there have to be a lot of "portable" toilets available. "Several weeks before the festival, a committee including police officers, firefighters, local government supervisors, and members of the festival committee walk the parade route to discuss what services are needed at the parade." During this walk, the locations for the restroom facilities are chosen.

Bonnie hires a company to provide 300 portable toilets. They put them up in several parks along the parade route. On the day of the parade, staff from the company clean up and keep the cubicles supplied. After the parade, the toilets are removed.

Activity

Produce a publicity poster

Prepare and distribute posters for an event that is being planned in your school.

1. Establish how much money is available for materials and copying. Collect all the information you'll need to include on the poster (answers to "Who?" "What?" "When?" Where?" and "How much?").
2. Produce a budget, showing how the money will be spent and how many copies you can produce for that amount.
3. Plan poster design.
4. Once the group approves your design and the budget, go for it! Produce the poster, make copies, and post them.

Challenge

Collect four or five posters from professional events. Analyze how effectively they communicate the mood or theme of the event. How would you improve them, for more effective advertising?

How to become a festival organizer

"My mother was a music instructor," recalls Bonnie. "So when I was growing up, I attended and participated in a lot of musical events. I'm sure this helped me. To do this kind of work, you have to understand and appreciate the reason for the occasion, and feel part of it."

Bonnie did well in school, and liked math and science as well as English and French. Before becoming a festival organizer, she worked in a government job and at an insurance company. She learned to do administrative work but was eager to move to a setting that she found more interesting. "When the job of organizing Caribana was advertised, I applied," she says. "I think I was hired because I had a lot of experience with artistic productions and I'm good at organizing people and information."

"I work with a lot of different people to get things done," she explains. "So, I have to know how to get along with people and accept them as they are. Artists especially have a reputation for being temperamental. It helps to understand their difficulties — artists have to get out of themselves and become different people on stage."

People interested in organizing cultural or community events also need practical skills in keeping track of information, planning, and budgeting. Business departments in colleges or universities offer courses in managing community events, but many other business courses would be useful as well.

Year-round special events

For any public event, preparations begin months in advance. Volunteers of all ages work on committees and help out during the event itself. There is no better way to learn about organizing than to be a volunteer. Find out about events in your community such as:

- Ice Sculpture Exhibition
- Chinese New Year Golden Dragon Parade
- Mardi Gras
- Earth Day
- a music festival
- Fall Fair
- a film festival
- New Year's Celebration

Is this career for you?

If you love the excitement of holiday celebrations, community festivals, or big sports events, this career may be for you.

As festival organizer, Bonnie uses both her knowledge of art and culture and her organizing abilities. "Usually events are organized by teams of volunteers who take care of different tasks," advises Bonnie. "But they also have to work closely together. The organizer needs to be patient and even-tempered and to make sure that everyone knows what everyone else is doing."

Organizing special events can be very exciting and lots of fun, but very demanding too. During the last few days before the event, it is not unusual for people to put in long hours and work late. On the day of the event, the festival organizer may be very tense, especially if some things

Costumes get more and more elaborate every year and costume design and preparations begin months ahead of the festival.

don't go as planned or new arrangements have to be made at the last minute. But there are often great parties at the end, where the organizers get to celebrate the results of all their work.

Career planning

Find out about an event that is being planned in your community. Volunteer your time on one of the committees. You may get valuable experience long before the event happens.

Contact the organizer of an upcoming event in your community. Ask if you can "job shadow" for half a day. Make notes, and photograph the different tasks done.

Making Career Connections

Ask a career counsellor about the courses that might help you become a festival coordinator or event manager. Write to the college asking about entrance requirements and job prospects for graduates.

Arrange to interview a volunteer who helped organize a large event. Ask what parts of the event turned out as expected, and if there were any problems or delays. Ask if there were "contingency plans" in case something went wrong.

Getting started

Interested in being a festival organizer? Here's what you can do now.
1. When you attend a large public event, think about how successful it was. How did people find out about it? Were the tickets a fair price? How could the organization be improved?
2. Keep a list of the events you attend and any special features you notice. This will remind you of things you can mention later in job interviews.
3. Take on a part-time job to get experience dealing with people.
4. Offer to coordinate an event for a group you belong to.
5. Learn to use a computer for text processing and to store and retrieve information.
6. In school, take language and arts courses to develop your communication skills. Math and science courses will help you learn how to organize information.

Related careers

Here are some related careers you may want to check out.
Public relations organizer
Helps companies and organizations deliver information to the public. Produces and distributes posters or flyers, buys advertising space in the media, and persuades the media to produce stories about the event.
Chef
Makes food for large numbers of people. Needs to know about menu planning, food purchasing, food preparation, and health standards.
Band leader
Organizes a group of musicians who play at public events. Needs to work closely with an agent or contacts in the community to get bookings for the band to perform.
Fund raiser
Works with corporations, institutions, and individuals, raising money for worthy causes. Needs excellent people skills and strong self-confidence.

Future watch

Bonnie is always answering questions from people in other cities interested in planning large cultural celebrations. The career of a festival organizer is quite new. Perhaps because there is so much home entertainment, with TVs, video, and computers, people like to get out occasionally to large special events. We can expect that events like the Caribana Festival that Bonnie coordinates will become more spectacular each year.

Tracy Macdonnell

Historical Interpreter

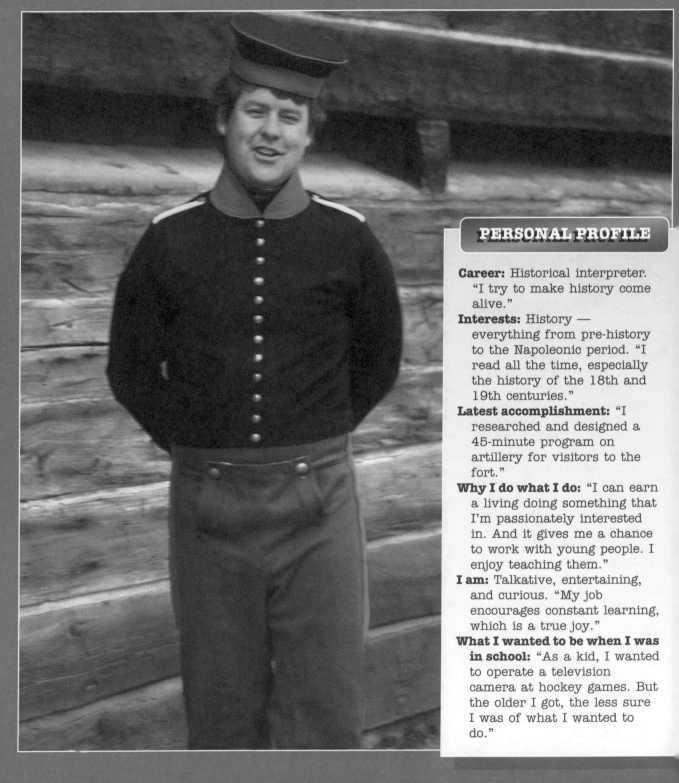

PERSONAL PROFILE

Career: Historical interpreter. "I try to make history come alive."

Interests: History — everything from pre-history to the Napoleonic period. "I read all the time, especially the history of the 18th and 19th centuries."

Latest accomplishment: "I researched and designed a 45-minute program on artillery for visitors to the fort."

Why I do what I do: "I can earn a living doing something that I'm passionately interested in. And it gives me a chance to work with young people. I enjoy teaching them."

I am: Talkative, entertaining, and curious. "My job encourages constant learning, which is a true joy."

What I wanted to be when I was in school: "As a kid, I wanted to operate a television camera at hockey games. But the older I got, the less sure I was of what I wanted to do."

What a historical interpreter does

Many historic sites have been restored to their original form, so that visitors can see how people lived and worked in years gone by. At many sites, historical interpreters, such as Tracy Macdonnell, dress in period costumes and guide the visitors around on tours. Tourists can see examples of the farms and houses where people lived, the mills and smithies where they worked, and the schools, churches, and stores where they gathered.

Tracy works at a fort that dates from the late 18th century. As a historical interpreter, he does his own research and designs programs to make history come alive for visitors. "We're called interpreters instead of guides because we each have our own presentation for tourists," he explains. "One of the great strengths of this place is that the same tour group or school class can visit the fort several times and learn something new each time."

Tracy's main area of interest is weaponry and military tactics. He may do some research at the fort itself or go off-site to a library, a university, or another historic site. "In my research, I often use a computer to search for information," he explains. "I might find what I need in books, magazines, journals, or on the Internet. Sometimes, I study objects such as clothing, furniture, and tools that the soldiers used almost 200 years ago."

Historical sleuthing

One of Tracy's most unusual searches sprang from a question asked by a boy on a recent tour of the fort. "He wanted to know what the soldiers and their families used for toilet paper. It was a great question, and one that had never

An early painting shows the fort where Tracy works. Wooden buildings in the early nineteenth century were made of logs. The fort was burned to the ground in 1812, rebuilt the following year, and restored as a historical site in 1934.

occurred to us before. We did a lot of investigation. Although we didn't come up with a definite answer, we think they probably used cloth rags."

When Tracy isn't researching or conducting tours, he's busy with administrative tasks such as ordering supplies, or developing new programs. "For my artillery program," he notes, "I studied an old three-volume manual on armaments. I borrowed it from a military college.

"The manual covered everything from making gunpowder to loading and firing a cannon. Then I designed an activity in which several teams of school kids competed to see who could load a cannon the fastest and most safely. Naturally, we used fake gunpowder."

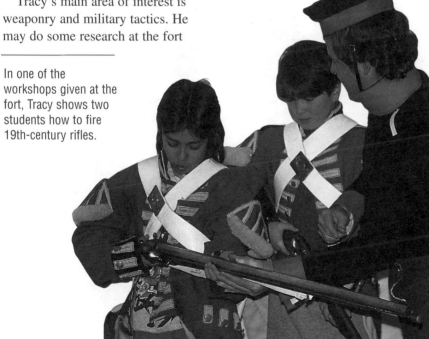

In one of the workshops given at the fort, Tracy shows two students how to fire 19th-century rifles.

All in a day's work

Tracy's day usually begins about 8:45 a.m. when he arrives at the fort for opening duties. He unlocks all of the buildings around the site, puts out the side arms (old muskets and revolvers) and gets his kit (his uniform) ready for the day.

"While I'm conducting tours I wear the uniform of a private of the 8th Regiment of Foot of the British Army," he explains. "I wear a red jacket, a set of white cross belts and a bayonet scabbard, grey overalls, black square-toed shoes, and a shako, which is a lacquered felt hat with a worsted wool tuft. In order to prepare my kit, I polish my shoes, clean my brass — the buttons on my jacket — and whiten my belts. I also wear two other uniforms, both blue."

During the school year, Tracy's weekday mornings typically begin with a workshop or a tour for a class of students. Tours cover everything from military music and muskets to the living conditions of the soldiers and their wives and children. The students visit the soldiers' barracks and the officers' quarters. This gives them a chance to compare the lifestyles of the two groups.

Separating fact from fiction

"There's a popular misconception that officers were fops and dandies who spent all their time socializing," says Tracy. "Actually, they were

professionals who worked very hard and lived in conditions that were not at all glamorous.

"Nevertheless," he adds, "the rank-and-file soldiers lived in far more severe surroundings. Their living conditions were very difficult. I try to get the students to imagine what it was like. These soldiers had enlisted — they weren't drafted. Why would someone choose to live that kind of a life?"

During the afternoon, Tracy does his research and paperwork. "I don't have an office, so I work wherever there's room.

The hands-on component is what makes historic sites so special. "Unlike in museums, where you're told not to touch anything, we encourage our visitors to pick things up and examine them," says Tracy. "This is the kind of place where you get to roll up your sleeves and muck around."

Who won the War of 1812?

Fort York, where Tracy works, is in the present-day city of Toronto, Ontario. The fort was the focus of two battles in the War of 1812 between Britain and the United States of America. After the Americans burned Fort York in 1812, the British retaliated by burning the White House in Washington.

Who won the war? Depending on which history books you read, you may have a different opinion. Both Americans and Canadians claim victory.

"We're also trained to work at other historic sites in case there's a staff shortage. So one or two days a month, I might work at the nearby Marine Museum, which covers the nautical history of the Great Lakes."

Tracy works an average of five days a week, which almost always includes at least one weekend day. Weekend visitors include youth groups, tourists, and the general public.

History in the rough

"Some amateur historians want to know what it was really like to live back then. We sometimes run special weekends during which these visitors, called 're-enactors,' wear

Detailed drawings like these are valued by historical researchers.

homemade costumes, camp in the field, eat in the soldiers' mess, and take part in field exercises and firing demonstrations. They experience things you can't get from books.

"Last year, I took part in a re-enactment of the battle of Stoney Creek, which took place in June, 1813. One night I went to bed with very wet feet. I knew they would feel even worse the next morning. I'd rarely been so miserable. And that's when it hit me — I thought, 'These people really lived like this!'"

What was it like to live in 1812? What would people who lived in 1812 think about our lives today?

Activity

Bringing history to life

To be a historical interpreter, you need a thorough knowledge of the time and place you're talking about. Here's an opportunity to practice your research skills.

1. Choose one subject area that interests you. You might pick
   • life in the military
   • farming methods
   • medicines and health
   • cooking
   • weapons
   • transportation
   • education
2. Select a time period and a location. Will you research France in the late 19th century, or 15th-century China?
3. Visit a library and learn all you can about the subject you've chosen. If you have access to the Internet, contact a re-enactors' group about the time you're researching.

4. Based on what you've learned, choose a job that you think you might enjoy. Imagine what it would be like to own a store, run a household or farm, or drive a carriage.

Challenge

Prepare a presentation for family or friends. You could:
• write and perform a play, enacting incidents in the daily life of the job you've chosen;
• have a friend play the part of a modern-day reporter, interviewing you about your daily life.

How to become a historical interpreter

Although history is his great love, Tracy's studies after high school focused on political science. After graduation, he wasn't sure what he wanted to do. "I spent the next five years doing a variety of jobs — everything from clerical work to making dirt in a potting soil factory," he laughs.

One day, Tracy found the classified section of a week-old newspaper, and saw an advertisement for the job of historical interpreter. "I figured they had probably filled the position but decided to apply anyway. I thought that at least I might get my name on a list for the next vacancy."

Tour groups can arrange to take part in a variety of presentations about the early 19th century. Baking bread for the household was a regular weekly chore then.

He was a little surprised to get a call inviting him in for an interview. The interview, he recalls, was unlike any other he'd ever had. "They were interested in finding out my opinions and interests. They were less concerned about my previous job experience than most employers would be." He was hired soon after.

Constant change

After several years on the job, Tracy says he realizes that things will never settle down to "normal." "That's the nature of this place. The only certainty is change."

One thing that's changed recently is that he does more paperwork now. "Because of budget cutbacks, we all have to pitch in and do more. Administration is really not my thing, although some of the other people here really enjoy it."

*I*s this career for you?

If you love history and enjoy working with groups of people, this might be the career for you. You'll need excellent communications skills, patience, and plenty of self-assurance.

"This is no job for a shy person or someone who's uncomfortable making public presentations," Tracy advises. "People who like predictability and a well-defined routine should also beware, because no two days are alike."

Tracy derives tremendous satisfaction from his work, especially because he works independently. But he's the first to admit that the job has its difficult moments.

Suspending disbelief

"Because we wear period costumes, the people who visit have to be willing to suspend disbelief, and go along with the roles we play. Most people are fine, but sometimes

When Tracy is not conducting tours, he spends time learning more about the 1800s.

you get a class where a few kids start making fun of the costumes. That spoils the mood a little."

"It's also frustrating that we can't do all the programs we'd like to," says Tracy. "This is because there's not enough money available. But we do the best we can with what we have.

"The main requirement for a historical interpreter," says Tracy, "is a love of the subject that constantly pushes you to learn more. You have to consider it an avocation, not just a nine-to-five job. I'm fortunate to be one of those people who likes bringing work home at the end of the day."

Career planning

Making Career Connections

Visit a tourist information office in your community. Ask for information about historical sites and re-enactments. Attend a re-enactment, if you can, and arrange to participate in the next one.

Call or write to your local historical board. Attend a meeting and find out about the projects in your community. Volunteer to help in one of them.

Arrange to interview a history teacher. Ask what led to that career choice, and what is liked and disliked about the job.

Visit a local museum or historic site and ask if you may job-shadow a historical interpreter for a day. Make notes and take pictures of the person at work.

Getting started

Interested in being a historical interpreter? Here's what you can do now.

1. Apply to work as a volunteer at a historic site or museum near your home.
2. Develop your communications skills, especially in public speaking. Join your school debating team or speak up at community events.
4. For dramatic historical presentations, some acting experience is an asset. You can gain this experience by joining your school drama club.
5. Keep a journal. Some of the best sources of information for historical researchers are the journals of ordinary people. Read a historic journal written in a time period that interests you. In your journal, record information such as the cost of food, your daily schedule, and how technology affects your life.

Related careers

Here are some related careers you may want to check out.

Information specialist
Helps users access library or archive resources. (An archive is a place where historic documents are kept.) Conducts reference searches.

Museum guide
Conducts tours of museum or gallery exhibitions and displays. Researches information about museum exhibits, and answers questions about them.

Curator
Researches the origins and history of objects displayed in museums and galleries. Develops the "story line" of displays and exhibitions.

Historic site administrator
Plans, organizes, and directs the activities of a historic site. Duties include developing policies and procedures, administering budgets, and developing promotional programs.

Future watch

There is a growing interest in preserving and maintaining local history and heritage sites. Interpreters who constantly expand their areas of interest and knowledge will be in demand. Tourists are increasingly fascinated by historic sites. They particularly like sites where the historical interpreters act exactly like people who lived in the past.

Meeting and Convention Planner

PERSONAL PROFILE

Career: Meeting and convention planner.

Interests: Music, dancing, entertaining, cross-country skiing, canoeing, and traveling. "I also get a lot of satisfaction from speaking to groups about coping with the loss of sight."

Latest accomplishment: Organizing a three-day conference in English and French for people from all over the U.S. and Canada. "I was also the keynote speaker."

Why I do what I do: "I like to begin a project and follow it through. It's a real thrill to bring together many individual details to create a successful event."

I am: "Energetic, compassionate, detail-oriented, and a perfectionist. I'm always striving to learn more — I have a real thirst for knowledge."

What I wanted to be when I was in school: "A teacher, like my mother and grandfather. In fact, I studied to be a teacher. And although I didn't follow that career path, I enjoy the fact that my work allows me to do some teaching."

What a meeting and convention planner does

Every year, millions of business meetings take place. They range from casual groups of half-a-dozen people meeting over muffins and coffee, to elaborate week-long events with detailed agendas (programs) and hundreds of people. All of these business meetings need to be planned. Dates, times, and places must be established, and the participants must be told these details. All this is the job of a meeting and convention planner such as Frances Tanner.

Some meeting and convention planners are freelancers who work for several clients. Others, like Frances, are employed by international companies to organize all their meetings and special events.

"I get requests from all over the company," she explains.

"They might want to talk about budgets or do some planning for the following year. I choose the site based on who the participants are, whether they know one another, how long the event lasts, and what they hope to achieve. I organize about 100 events a year.

"I usually hear about an event two weeks in advance," notes Frances. "But I start organizing a large event such as a conference as much as a year before."

On other occasions, however, she has to put something together on very short notice. "If they spring something on me, I just have to do my best," she says. "Recently I was asked to put together a wedding shower on five hours' notice. I called a nearby caterer for the food, got decorations from a supplier in our building and asked the host to issue the invitations. It was a big success and everyone enjoyed themselves."

All the details

The planner is responsible for every detail of the meeting. Frances arranges everything from audiovisual equipment to refreshments. "I send out invitations, design and decorate meeting rooms, prepare information kits — you name it, I do it," she laughs.

"I get a lot of help ahead of time from the staff at my office," she says. "At the meeting site I rely on the people who work for the hotel or convention center."

Meeting planners spend a lot of time researching facilities such as hotels, restaurants, and convention sites. "I meet frequently with representatives from the facilities that would like our business," Frances says. "I ask them about details such as the size and layout of the meeting rooms, menu selections, and costs."

Frances organizes dozens of meetings, parties, and special events every year. Up to the day of the event, guest lists must be checked, meeting rooms booked, and menus updated. The computer helps Frances keep track of all the details and insure that things run smoothly.

Frances checks over a menu with a representative from a large hotel. "By getting to know the suppliers on a first-name basis, we can all do our jobs better," she comments.

All in a day's work

Frances arrives at work about 8:30 a.m. with her guide dog, Jilly. She checks for any material that may have arrived overnight. "People sometimes leave printed material on my chair or desk. I go over that first, then turn on the computer to check my electronic mail. After that I get my faxes and overnight mail, then listen to my telephone voice mail."

If an event is scheduled in the next three days, Frances pulls its file and updates it. She notes all updated information on her computer and prints a hard copy for the file. "It takes a lot of paper so I always recycle."

Then, she reviews the bills from recent meetings. It's up to Frances to ensure that the costs are in line with those in the budget. Once she approves them, she sends the bills to the event host (the person who called the meeting) for payment.

Because of her blindness, Frances's job presents her with some special challenges. Frances's files are all clearly marked in Braille with the name of the events she's working on. She spends several hours a day using a computer with a "voice." This tells her what is on the screen. An optical scanner translates printed material into Braille so she can read it. Because the scanner doesn't read glossy paper or anything written in italics, Frances relies on other people to read these materials to her.

It's not unusual for Frances to have several phone messages waiting for her each morning. If she leaves her office for a brief coffee break, she often returns to 15 or more. "I sometimes feel like I spend my life on the phone," she laughs.

Inspections

After lunch, Frances does a site inspection of local facilities where upcoming events are scheduled. "I do an inspection about every three weeks," she explains. "I meet with the hotel's sales director, the front-desk manager, the catering coordinator, and the audiovisual person. I tell the staff our needs, and they advise me about any possible problems so we can solve them before the event."

After many years in the business, Frances knows the dimensions of the meeting rooms she has previously used, their layout, and the number of people they hold. "When I discuss a new facility with the hotel staff, we review the floor plans," she explains. "This is one of the most difficult parts of my job for me. My assistant helps to orient me by tracing an outline of the floor plan on my hand with her finger. And when I visit a new location for the first time, she

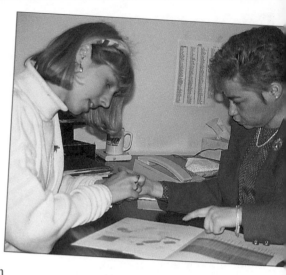

When Frances is considering using an unfamiliar space, she asks her assistant to trace an outline of the room's floor plan on her hand so that she understands its layout.

accompanies me and traces the outline of the site on my back."

Going to a meeting

Frances or one of her staff usually attends each event. "We don't actually sit in on the meetings," she explains, "but we're busy 'behind the scenes.'" Frances arrives early to

make sure that all is ready. During the event, she checks that refreshments are ready for the breaks, and that microphones or projectors are available. She also ensures that participants receive any important phone or fax messages.

Trouble shooting

Meeting and convention planners must constantly update and revise their plans as they receive new information. Frances recently planned a meeting that 100 people were expected to attend. About a week in advance, only half that number had said they would be there. She had to cancel half of the room bookings at the hotel and advise the caterer that fewer people would require meals.

Occasionally, says Frances, an event is suddenly cancelled. "Cancellations are the worst thing that can happen, especially if it's only a day or two before the event is scheduled to take place. Fortunately, that's rare. However, sometimes an event is postponed by several weeks or even months. That means we have to start planning again from scratch."

Follow-up

A key part of any event is the evaluation that takes place afterward. Frances asks the host to do an assessment and also conducts her own. The information is then passed on to the management of the facility where it took place. "I always give them my feedback. If I don't tell them what I think, they won't know what to improve for next time."

MEETING EVENT GUIDELINE

This guideline is provided as a checklist for our upcoming meeting. Please complete the following questions to facilitate the coordination of your event. Upon receipt, I will be calling you in order to review this checklist and discuss any additional details.

Company/Division:

Contact Name:

Phone Number:

Name of Meeting:

1. In what city is your meeting to take place?
2. In what part of the city would you prefer your meeting to be located?

☐ Near Office ☐ Near Airport ☐ 1/hr from City ☐ Other

Site Selection Deadline

3. What range of dates are you interested in:
   What is the preferred date:
4. How many participants do you expect?
5. Of the total participants mentioned above, how many will require accommodation?

☐ Single (1 Per room) ☐ Double (2 Per room)

6. Which method of hotel reservations would interest you the most:

Activity

Plan your own meeting

Organizing meetings and special events requires good planning skills and the ability to delegate responsibilities to others. This activity will help you to understand the steps involved in planning and carrying out a successful meeting.

Ask your teacher for permission to organize a class meeting to discuss setting up an environmental committee at school.

1. Decide on the purpose of your committee. Give yourselves goals. For example, list three outcomes you wish to achieve.
2. Next, choose the time and place for the meeting. How much time do you have for the meeting? Can you use your regular classroom or would it be better to hold it elsewhere — the lunch room or the library, for instance?
3. Set the agenda. Ask your teacher and classmates for suggestions.

Find out how many of your classmates are interested. Remember that you have limited time for the meeting and keep the number of items within reason. Put the most important goals first.

4. Make copies of the agenda, including the meeting date, time, and location, and distribute them to your teacher and classmates. Ask a classmate to keep track of those who will attend and update the list just before the meeting, so you know how many to expect.
5. Decide who will best run the meeting. The chairperson must make sure that things move smoothly and that all (or, at least, most) of the agenda is covered.
6. Will you be using videotapes, audiotapes, or overheads during the meeting? If so, you need to arrange for special equipment. Ask someone in the class to get the equipment and be responsible for

Make a checklist, like the one above for every meeting and special event you plan. be sure to update it regularly and check that each item is being taken care of.

setting it up, operating it, and returning it.

7. Before the meeting, ask someone to take simple minutes. You don't need to write down every word spoken but you need to note the major items discussed, the decisions made, and who is to follow up with action. Afterward make sure minutes are circulated to everyone who attended.
8. Put someone in charge of making sure that the room is left tidy at the end.
9. The final step is following up. Did you decide to establish an environmental committee? If so, will you make a presentation to the student council?

How to become a meeting and convention planner

Frances first worked in the tourism and hospitality industry as a high school student. She spent several summers as a tour guide at Niagara Falls where she discovered that she loved working with many different people.

She enrolled in a hotel management program after high school. "Many colleges offer these," she notes. Frances spent the next two summers working as the front-desk clerk at a 19-room inn. "I did everything from bookings and cancellations to housekeeping management," she recalls. "It gave me a real feel for the hospitality industry."

Following graduation, Frances worked as a conference organizer for the college she had attended. "That experience," she says, "was the best possible preparation for my current job. The work was very similar to what I'm doing now, and I was out meeting new people all the time."

Creating her own job — twice

Ten years ago, Frances lost her sight due to illness. Concerned that blindness would prevent her from finding work in her chosen field, she decided to create her own job. "I worked as an information officer with a national organization that provides support and services for people who are visually impaired. I presented lectures on the abilities of visually impaired people to groups all over the country."

About five years ago, Frances realized that she missed working in the hospitality industry. She wrote to her present employer about working as a full-time meeting and convention planner. "It was a huge company that held hundreds of meetings all over the world every year. However, they had never employed anyone just to plan those meetings. I knew it was a good idea so I developed a job description and sold them on it. Again, I created my own job!"

Now, many companies employ meeting and convention planners. "We're an essential part of the business world," Frances says.

Is this career for you?

Imagination and creativity are great assets in meeting and convention planners. "I'm constantly challenged to come up with fresh, new ideas for events. At last year's staff winter party," Frances recalls, "I borrowed an old two-runner sleigh and set it up as a backdrop for photos. People loved it!"

It's important to be able to focus on small details, such as having paper and pens on the meeting tables. At the same time, you must be able to step back and look at how the details fit into the whole picture.

Close attention to detail is a vital part of a meeting and convention planner's work.

"Of course, you also need great organizational skills," adds Frances. "With more than 100 events to plan every year, there's a lot of overlap. I have to keep the details of each one on track."

The job requires a lot of flexibility and a willingness to work long hours, including weekends. Many events are held in the evening, and Frances often has to check with airports and hotels late at night to confirm the arrival of important visitors.

"This is no job for a nine-to-five person," she advises. "It's also hard on a worrier, which I am. You feel responsible for ensuring that everything goes well."

Career planning

Making Career Connections

Job shadow someone who works with food, such as a caterer. Note how many roles he or she must play: estimating amounts, ordering and preparing food, knowing about food safety, pricing, advertising, serving, to name just a few.

Talk to a parent or teacher who has volunteered to organize a meeting. Find out what was involved and ask how the event went. What did they like about the experience? What would they do differently another time?

Try to get a summer job in the tourism field, as a tour guide or in a restaurant or hotel. This will give you some insight into how the industry works.

Find out whether your school or community center rents meeting space to outside groups. If so, what does it cost to rent space for a meeting? How much advance notice do they require? How many people can be accommodated?

Getting started

Interested in being a meeting and convention planner? Here's what you can do now.

1. Volunteer to help organize your school's next big event, such as a dance or concert. Take charge of one specific area, such as decorating or refreshments. Organize a committee to help you.
2. Try to get a summer job in the tourism field, as a tour guide or in a restaurant or hotel.
3. Get involved in your school's student government. Help to organize the next set of elections, or manage the campaign of someone running for office.
4. Take mathematics, business, computer, and communication courses in high school. Travel and tourism and design classes also help. The more aspects of the business you understand, the better prepared you'll be.

Related careers

Here are some related careers you may want to check out.

Recreation director
Organizes and carries out special activities at a resort or on a cruise ship. Promotes and publicizes the events.

Hotel manager
Manages all aspects of the day-to-day operation of a hotel or resort. Responsible for managing all staff and ensuring that the hotel provides a high standard of service.

Caterer
Works for a hotel or meeting facility, or freelance. Responsible for all aspects of planning, preparing, and serving meals and refreshments to guests.

Rental services provider
Rents tables, chairs, cutlery, dishes, decorations, etc. to people planning parties and meetings. Often advises clients on other services such as caterers and florists.

Future watch

Many companies trying to cut back on expenses are reducing their travel budgets significantly. As a result, a growing number of business meetings are taking place via teleconference and video conference. "Planners of such meetings need to know how to use complex new technologies involving computers and telecommunications," Frances cautions.

Smaller companies often hire freelance consultants who provide similar services for a group of clients. These consultants own their own businesses and offer a full range of services to several firms at a time.

Dawn and Wally Tabobondung

Marina Operators

PERSONAL PROFILE

Career: Marina operators. "It's a great life for people who like the outdoors and want to be near the water."

Interests: Outdoor activities — swimming, baseball, fishing, boating, and snowmobiling. Dawn enjoys reading books and magazines when she has the time. "I like both nonfiction and fiction, especially mysteries."

Latest accomplishment: Staging a rock concert. "It was such a success that we've built a stage as part of a year-round entertainment area nearby."

Why we do what we do: "We love working with people and we love the outdoors. It's the best of both worlds."

I am: Dawn: "Friendly and hard working. I like a challenge and this is the most challenging work I've ever done." Wally: Easygoing and patient. "I really enjoy working with my hands."

What I wanted to be when I was in school: Dawn: "To work in the tourism and hospitality industry." Wally: "I wanted to have my own construction business."

What a marina operator does

Dawn and Wally Tabobondung are a brother-and-sister team who manage a marina complex located on a large island. The marina consists of docking for about 75 boats, a restaurant with takeout service, and a small store. Nearby is a large park where they recently held a rock concert. The marina, the park, and 50 campsites are on aboriginal land, owned by their native band.

Much of Dawn's and Wally's work goes on outside. "We service and fuel boats, help people set up camp, repair docks, and so on," explains Dawn. "We also sell convenience store items — canned food, household necessities, and snacks — as well as fuel, maps, and fishing gear and licenses."

A four-season operation

The marina operates year-round but the busy season is from May to September when boating, diving, camping, and fishing are at their peak. "It can be tough to see everyone out there enjoying the beautiful weather when we have to work," admits Dawn. "We have to be willing to give up our summer."

"During peak season," Wally adds, "the marina is open seven days a week. In spring and fall we open Friday through Monday. From November to February, we open only on weekends to accommodate ice fishermen and year-round cottagers." During the winter, the Tabobondungs maintain a skating rink and sled runs and provide indoor activities, such as billiards and other games.

Motorboats are a major source of pollution in North American lakes. Great care is needed when fueling them because of the risk of gasoline leaks and spills.

How to reduce oil and gasoline spills

One of the main issues discussed at a marina operators' conference that Dawn and Wally attended was the problem of gasoline and oil spills.

The marina sells about 150 000 L (40 000 U.S. gallons) of gasoline each year. Wally estimates that each time a motorboat fills up, about half a cup of fuel spills into the bay. "Even though we're careful, spills still happen. When you multiply half a cup of gasoline times thousands of fill-ups a year, you get an idea of the extent of the problem."

Wally has learned some simple, practical ways to reduce gasoline spills. One of the easiest is to use a funnel, which controls the flow of fuel into the tank. An alternative for smaller boats is to remove the tank from the boat so that the pump's nozzle can be inserted directly into it.

Like all people who make their living near water, Wally and Dawn are concerned about the state of the environment. They know that taking good care of the land and water makes good economic as well as scientific sense.

Wally takes part in government-sponsored environmental assessments and cleanup operations. "Right now I'm working with the band on an environmental study of the island," he says. "I've lived here most of my life. This is also my children's home and it's important to me that the area stays clean and healthy."

All in a day's work

During the summer season, Wally and Dawn arrive at work about 7 a.m. They open up the store, put on a pot of coffee, and prepare to greet the first customers of the day. They don't have long to wait. Fishermen, in particular, start the day very early — often as the sun rises.

"One of the things that makes this job so enjoyable is the variety of people you meet," says Dawn. "They come in to eat or shop, and wind up chatting, exchanging local gossip, and swapping tall tales. You get to know the regulars very well and there are some real characters!"

No two days are alike and the only certainty for the Tabobondungs is the long hours. During July and August, the marina is open until 11 p.m. and Dawn and Wally rarely get away from work except to sleep. "And not much of that, either," says Wally, who has two young children.

"It's important to have a good attitude when you're dealing with the public," says Dawn. "I really hate to see money walking away because of poor service."

Sharing the load

The Tabobondungs divide the workload between them. Dawn looks after the convenience store — ordering, stocking shelves, and overseeing the restaurant and food service area — while Wally operates the marina.

"During the busy months, says Dawn, "the store and restaurant are also staffed by two other band members. They prepare and serve the food and look after the cash register. I run the store and restaurant by myself the rest of the year."

Since the marina doesn't have any space for an office, Dawn set one up at home. Here, she takes care of the paperwork, including budgeting, accounting, invoicing, and bookkeeping. Paperwork can take her about eight hours a week. "We recently computerized our bookkeeping system, which makes it a lot easier to keep track of finances

Recently, Dawn and Wally staged a rock concert in the park beside the marina. "It was a big success," says Dawn, "despite the fact that it was probably the worst weekend of the summer. We weren't sure if the musicians would play because it was storming so badly. But they braved the weather and we got a crowd of about 1200 people."

It's a Fact

Almost three quarters of the Earth is covered by water. How much of it is fresh water like that in lakes and streams? Only 2.5% – the rest is salt water! Marinas serve boats on all major waterways.

and maintain a good cash flow," she says. "That was an important step forward."

The outside is Wally's domain — he drives the water taxi (taking people to cottages they can't reach by car), organizes fishing trips and tourist excursions, fuels boats, and delivers groceries and propane to cottagers. He also maintains the marina property, cutting the grass, painting, and making repairs as needed.

During the off-season there's less outdoor work at the marina, except for shovelling snow. Wally does repairs, builds docks, and plows snow for some of the cottagers. He also operates a winter storage facility for boats.

Winter fishing in the frozen north

A main attraction of ice fishing is that you don't need an expensive boat and equipment. The two things you need are very thick, safe ice (at least 20 cm or 8 inches thick) and to be with an experienced adult. Together, you can walk to a likely spot, cut a hole in the ice, and drop your baited hook through. You might also use a sled for dragging equipment onto the ice, a bait bucket to bring home the catch, and a short fishing rod known as a jig stick. Light fishing line is advisable because heavy line freezes and becomes brittle, like wire.

Anything you use during the day — paper cups, cans, and so on — should be gathered up and taken back to shore for disposal. That's a good way of showing respect for the natural world.

To fish through the ice, you drill holes and put fishing lines through them. If you have a "tip-up," you'll know when you've got a bite on the line because a small flag pops up when the fish tugs on it.

Activity

Water: how much do you use?

We often take for granted the abundance of clean water. We use a lot of it for everything from cooking to brushing our teeth. Because it's so plentiful, it's easy to use a lot of water without really thinking about it.

The Tabobondungs get their water from Georgian Bay, a large bay on Lake Huron, one of the Great Lakes. Since they have to pump water from the bay and then filter it, they are careful to limit their usage to what they really need.

To get an idea of how much water you and your family use in a day, try keeping track of it. Use the chart shown to help you. Don't forget to calculate the water you use in cooking meals. You'll be surprised at the results.

Activity	Volume in liters	in U.S. gallons
Brushing your teeth (with the water running)	7.5	2
Flushing the toilet	26	7
Taking a bath	380	100
Taking a 10-minute shower (with a regular shower head)	225	60
Taking a 10-minute shower (with a water-saving shower head)	95	25
Washing the dishes in an automatic dishwasher	45	12
Drinking a glass of water (running the water to get it cold)	2	0.5
Drinking a glass of water (using an ice cube to get it cold)	0.3	0.1
Washing clothes in an automatic washing machine	75	20

How to become a marina operator

"There are many avenues into this field," explains Dawn. "In our case, we worked here for several years as students and helped the previous manager run the place. We already knew the business from top to bottom, were familiar with the clientele, and knew that we liked the work."

Dawn took accounting and computing courses in school and worked in restaurants and hotels. Wally studied to be a drafting technician and worked as a construction worker, contractor, and carpenter. He also served on the band council for four years and chaired the band's recreation committee.

For many years, the band had run the marina. Recently, however, the council decided that the marina would be more successful if managed privately. The Tabobondungs were very excited when the band invited interested groups to "bid" for the opportunity to run the place. They developed a long-term business plan, and the band council accepted their bid.

The first thing they did was to offer a discount on dock fees to all customers who paid in advance. This way, they were able to raise the funds they needed to buy supplies for their first season. It also meant they didn't have to go to the bank for a loan. "That helped to get us off to a good start," comments Dawn.

Measuring their success

After two years as marina operators, Dawn and Wally are pleased with the progress they've made. "The marina has been self-supporting since we took it over," notes Dawn, proudly. "We've made a go of it financially by watching every penny."

"If we give our hearts and souls to this place for the next five years," adds Wally, "we should be able to slow down a little and hire other people to handle more of the workload."

Kayaking gives a welcome break from a long day's work at a marina – when you can spare the time.

Is this career for you?

Do you like the water? Do you enjoy working with your hands? Are you a self-starter? Then this might be the job for you.

Energy and stamina are important because during the peak season, the days are very long and you rarely get a day off. "After July 1, I don't have any free time until after Labor Day," laments Wally. "Last summer I managed to go fishing twice in June and that was it until the fall."

You don't need a college degree or diploma to run a marina. However, you do need a lot of drive and determination, because you're working for yourself. And understanding business and small engine mechanics would certainly come in handy.

Bad weather can be a drawback to the job. During the winter months, it's common for the thermometer to register well below the freezing mark for weeks on end. Icy winds often make it feel much colder. "You have to like the outdoors," Wally says. "Even then, there are some days you'd rather just stay home."

The financial rewards are modest. "If you're hoping to get rich, look for a different job," Wally grins. What you will get is the chance to work in beautiful, natural surroundings and the sense of independence and satisfaction that comes from being your own boss.

Career planning

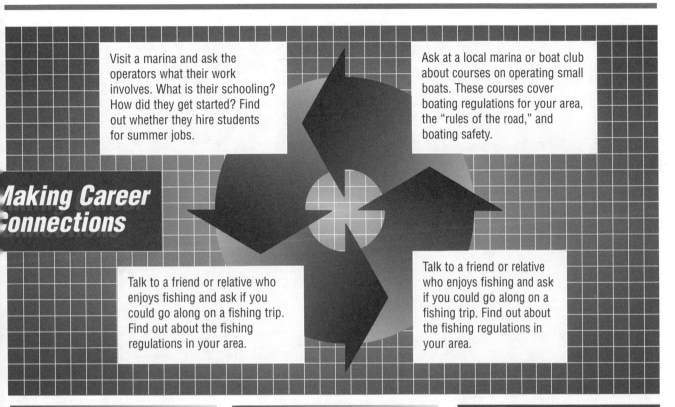

Visit a marina and ask the operators what their work involves. What is their schooling? How did they get started? Find out whether they hire students for summer jobs.

Ask at a local marina or boat club about courses on operating small boats. These courses cover boating regulations for your area, the "rules of the road," and boating safety.

Making Career Connections

Talk to a friend or relative who enjoys fishing and ask if you could go along on a fishing trip. Find out about the fishing regulations in your area.

Talk to a friend or relative who enjoys fishing and ask if you could go along on a fishing trip. Find out about the fishing regulations in your area.

Getting started

Interested in being a marina operator? Here's what you can do now.

1. Take courses in cardiopulmonary resuscitation (CPR) and first aid at your school or recreation center. These will help you cope in an emergency.
2. Become a good swimmer and take lifesaving courses at a local pool.
3. Read books and magazines on boating, fishing, and outdoor living.
4. Join an orienteering group to learn how to find your way with just a compass.
5. Help with repairs, cleanup, and painting around your home. Maintenance is a large part of running a marina.
6. In high school, take English, math, science, and business courses. These will help you no matter what job you do.

Related careers

Here are some related careers you may want to check out.

Fishing guide
Knows and understands the habits of fish. Plans and leads fishing trips for groups of people, showing them where the "big ones" should be.

Wilderness outfitter
Teaches people how to operate boats, including canoes and kayaks. Leads boating trips. Rents and sells a wide range of outdoor equipment: canoes, paddles, backpacks, tents, lifejackets, and more.

Lock operator
Opens and closes locks in canals. Many waterways for pleasure craft have canals and locks that are operated in the summer for touring boaters.

Swimming teacher
Works with individuals and groups of all ages from beginners to experienced swimmers. Must be an excellent swimmer and know lifesaving techniques.

Future watch

"Marinas have a great future," says Wally, "because tourism is such a vital part of North American life." Vacations in natural surroundings are particularly appealing because of their relatively low cost and simplicity. Also, people who live in cities like to "get away from it all" on their holidays. It's important for marina operators to understand the environmental issues that affect fish and the water. Many government environmental regulations are becoming stricter, and boaters and marina operators will have to comply.

John McComber

Guest Services Manager

PERSONAL PROFILE

Career: Guest services manager. "I began as a part-time bellhop when I was a student and stayed on when full-time work came along. It was just a summer job at first, but I enjoyed the hotel business."

Interests: "I'm an avid golfer, and I enjoy theater, movies, reading, and writing. In fact, right now I'm writing a novel set in the hotel industry.

Latest accomplishment: "I was recently promoted from chief concierge to guest services manager."

Why I do what I do: "I have a genuine interest in pleasing guests, in breaking down the barriers and getting to know people."

I am: Trustworthy and honest. "I also love a good sense of humor and enjoy the absurd."

What I wanted to be when I was in school: "I studied political science and law and thought I might become a journalist."

What a guest services manager does

John McComber is the guest services manager of a 380-room hotel. He hires, trains, schedules, and supervises about 40 people who take care of guests: drivers, the door and front desk staff, bellhops, and concierges. In hotel lingo, these people work in the "front-of-the-house" area, and John is called the "front-of-the-house manager." (The kitchen and the house-keeping, engineering, and laundry areas are behind the scenes and are called "back-of-the-house.")

John as concierge

Before becoming guest services manager, John was a concierge for 13 years. He knows the job well and understands just how important it is in a large hotel.

When he was a concierge, John had to deal with unusual, even bizarre, requests. Once, a guest wanted to play a practical joke on someone in another city. The guest asked John to have a jar of smoke delivered to that person! "We're used to hearing odd requests," says John matter-of-factly.

Another time, a musician who was a hotel guest asked for a massage mitt made of rabbit fur to ease aching muscles. John contacted one of the massage therapists on staff, who put him in touch with a supplier.

Whatever the guest's request, a concierge needs to be good at doing practical research on a moment's notice. "If you don't know the answer, you have to be able to find the answer as quickly as possible," says John. And if you're wondering how John delivered the smoke in a bottle, he says it wasn't as difficult as it seems. "We work closely with our colleagues," he says, "and rely on a worldwide network." He simply called another member of the Golden Keys Society in the other city who looked after it!

What is a concierge?

The word "concierge" (pronounced kon-see-erzh) comes from France, where it used to mean a doorkeeper or porter. Now used around the world, the word refers to hotel staff who help guests get the services they need. Do you want tickets to a concert in the city you are traveling to tomorrow? Are you looking for a vegetarian restaurant for dinner? Do you need some prescription medicine or emergency dental treatment? Don't worry — the hotel concierge will help you with dizzying efficiency.

You can recognize experienced concierges by the tiny crossed golden keys they wear on their lapels. After five years of work, they are eligible to join the Golden Key Society, an international association of concierges based in Paris, France.

Always in the public eye, concierges must have appealing personalities and appearances that invite guests to approach.

All in a day's work

At 8:30 every morning, John's day starts with a planning session. He meets with the hotel manager, the manager of housekeeping services, the food and beverage manager, the human resources manager, and the front-desk manager. "We review what's going to happen that day: how many guests are booked, what conferences are happening, and what regular guests we expect."

Then John meets with the front-of-the-house staff to tell them what groups or familiar guests to expect. "I make sure there are enough staff on duty to handle any large groups," says John.

Every other Wednesday, all the department heads in the hotel get together for an operations meeting to check that procedures are working well. Beyond that, there's little predictability in the hotel business. Every day is different but John enjoys the lack of routine.

"The most important thing to realize about this business," he explains, "is that the hotel never closes. There may be slow

A large part of John's day is spent talking with staff to make sure they have all the information and help they need to do their jobs well.

periods — winter is usually less busy than the summer when many guests come on vacation. But the hotel is open 24 hours a day, 365 days a year."

Weekends are often the busiest times. "I don't work on a schedule," comments John. "When the hotel's busy, I know I should be there." In a recent 10-day period, John had only one day off. "I'm not really single," he jokes. "I'm married to the hotel."

Humor helps

There is sometimes a lot of pressure, especially when John's staff gets several requests at the same time. John finds that humor helps get him and his staff through the day. In a red

There's a manual for every job in the hotel, listing the tasks each staff member is expected to do.

binder behind his desk, he and his staff record their most embarrassing or hilarious encounters.

One of John's funniest stories is of a Spanish-speaking guest who came up to John saying "*Aloma payamas*." Thinking it was a greeting, John cheerfully smiled back, repeating "*Aloma payamas*." But a Spanish-speaking staff member who overheard the conversation realized that the guest was trying to say, "I lost my pyjamas." The pyjamas had accidentally been taken to the laundry with the bedsheets. They were quickly found and all was well. Since then, the phrase *aloma payamas* has become a joke among John's staff — they use it regularly to say good night to each other!

Hiring new staff

John works with the hotel's human resources department to find and hire new staff. "Any staff member in my area must have a second language," says John. He speaks French, some Spanish, and some Italian along with English. When John is hiring, he looks at the language skills each person brings to the team. Among them, his six concierges can speak French, Spanish, German, Italian, Japanese, Cantonese, and Mandarin.

"I like to hire someone who is relaxed, sociable, and good at figuring out what people need," explains John. "What I really look for is personality. The person should be instinctively in tune with other people, to know what to offer and what not to offer."

Getting in the groove

When new employees begin, they spend the first day or two in an office, away from guests, reading a manual. "It is written like a textbook," says John. "The manual also tells about the company that owns the hotel and its philosophy. By reading it, new staff can understand the hotel's standards of service."

Once they've read the manual, they are assigned to job-shadow someone who is experienced at the work they'll be doing. During their first few days, they wear a name tag that says "trainee" so that guests know they are new on the job. "When I'm satisfied that they've learned the basics, we take the 'trainee' badge off," says John. "The training period usually lasts two to three days for door and bell staff, but longer — about a month — for a concierge. That's because the job is more complicated."

It's a Fact

Some airlines offer incentives to travel and tourism students such as a free return airline ticket for a job interview anywhere in the country. If you graduate from a travel and tourism course after high school, you could become eligible.

What is a bellhop?

A bellhop takes guests to their rooms, carries baggage, and delivers messages to the rooms. The word "bellhop" comes from the time before electricity was installed in hotels. Each room had a cord that was attached to a bell near the front desk. The guest pulled the cord which rang the bell. The bellhop saw which bell was ringing, and "hopped to it" to give service to the guest!

Activity

Planning a trip

Imagine that a pen pal from a different country is coming to visit your town or city for the first time. Your school has agreed to arrange for a three-day trip and cover the costs. Your visitor is interested in seeing your school but wants to see the local attractions as well and get a feel for life in your town or city.

Plan the best time of year to visit, which events to attend, and which sights to see.

- Draw a map of your town or city and mark on it your own favorite sites.
- Find out the costs of hotel accommodations and meals for three days.
- Prepare a detailed schedule, noting where you and your friend will be each morning, afternoon, and evening, what the two of you will do, and who will act as a guide.
- Calculate the total cost of the trip, including accommodation, meals, tickets, and transportation.

How to become a guest services manager

After they graduated from high school, many hotel staff took courses in hotel management at college. This program teaches the business end of running a hotel, how to attract guests, and how to train staff.

John, however, entered the hotel business from a different route. He studied political science and law after high school and was going to become a journalist. But after working at a hotel one summer, he changed his career plans. "I found that my general knowledge and research skills were useful when I started working as a concierge," he says.

John often makes suggestions to guests who want to know about nearby restaurants and sights.

John began as a bellhop, then was an assistant concierge for five years. He then became chief concierge, and is now a manager after 14 years. Some hotels like John's prefer to promote staff from within the hotel, provided the person is qualified. This policy benefits those who begin in the hotel business at the most junior jobs, such as bellhops or messengers. It's possible to work up from there, gaining useful experience in many different jobs.

Is this career for you?

Front-of-the-house hotel staff must pay careful attention to their appearance. It also helps if you are patient and considerate, even when guests are rude or grumpy. Practice listening carefully to what people are asking for, even when they are not really sure what they want. If you get satisfaction from making people feel comfortable and at home, hotel management could be a good field for you.

"Jobs such as bellhop and messenger require little training or experience and are ideal starting positions," advises John. "When you are able to juggle several different situations at the same time, you may be ready for promotion to the front desk. If you want to become a manager, you'll need skills in organization and administration.

"You have to react and decide in seconds how to help someone," he adds. "Resourcefulness and imagination are important. If you don't know an answer, you have to be able to find it as quickly as possible. That's the type of person I look for when I hire."

Hello, bonjour, moshi moshi!

John's staff can say hello (and much more) in:

Spanish	hola	o-la
French	bonjour	bonzhoor
Italian	buon giorno	boo-on jorno
German	guten tag	goo-ten takh
Mandarin	喂，你好嗎？	way nee how ma
Cantonese	喂，你好嗎？	way nay ho ma
Japanese	もしもし	moshi moshi

Career planning

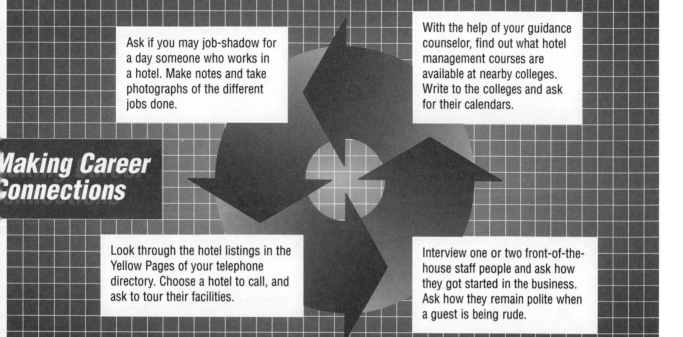

Ask if you may job-shadow for a day someone who works in a hotel. Make notes and take photographs of the different jobs done.

With the help of your guidance counselor, find out what hotel management courses are available at nearby colleges. Write to the colleges and ask for their calendars.

Making Career Connections

Look through the hotel listings in the Yellow Pages of your telephone directory. Choose a hotel to call, and ask to tour their facilities.

Interview one or two front-of-the-house staff people and ask how they got started in the business. Ask how they remain polite when a guest is being rude.

Getting started

Interested in being a guest services manager? Here's what you can do now.

1. The next time your family has overnight guests, help as a host. Plan their visit and try to anticipate what they need to be comfortable.
2. In the summer, try to get a part-time job pumping gas, serving tables in a restaurant, or working as a cashier, in order to practice taking care of customers.
3. Develop your ability to "read" people by paying close attention to their behavior in public places such as restaurants and malls.
4. Study your town or city so you could help tourists find their way around. Know where the theaters, sports centers, museums, and shopping areas are located.
5. In high school, take languages, and business and communications courses.

Related careers

Here are some related careers you may want to check out.

Front-desk clerk
Checks guests into their rooms, gives them their keys, checks them out, and collects payment. Must always know which rooms are still available.

Hotel messenger
Delivers mail, messages, dry cleaning, or other services to guests. Is always on the run.

Housekeeper
Cleans guest rooms. Arranges for clothes to be dry cleaned or laundered and shoes to be shined.

Server
Serves customers in restaurants. Hotel servers also take room-service meals to guests in their rooms.

Future watch

All hotel staff will need to be comfortable working with computer programs to make and change bookings and check information. They will also be expected to learn new systems as they are introduced.
Some hotel chains are now using interactive videodiscs to train new employees. These programs help trainees learn different aspects of their job, and quiz them on how they would handle different situations.

Lois Wong

Travel Agent

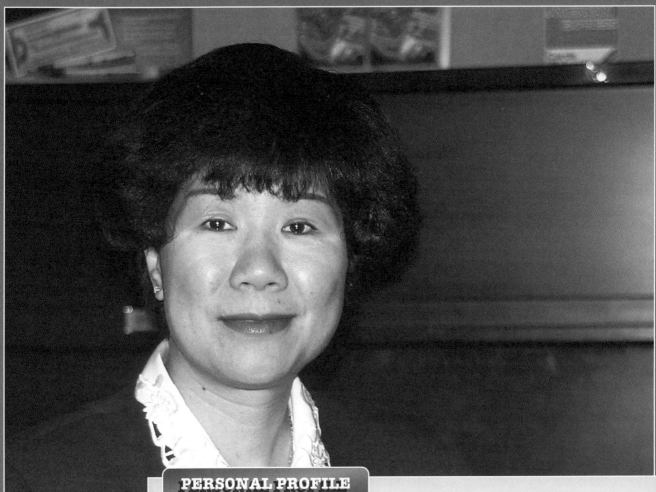

PERSONAL PROFILE

Career: Travel agent. "Do you like to travel? Do you want to see the world? If you also like helping people, then this is the job for you."

Interests: "I used to like traveling during my time off. But now that I've been around the world a few times, I find that I enjoy simply relaxing at home."

Latest accomplishment: Being her company's top earner for eight years in a row and receiving their Customer Care Award. "People are so nice! Some of my clients have written wonderful letters about me to head office."

Why I do what I do: "I love to travel and I love working with people face to face."

I am: "A happy and friendly person. If my clients are happy, I'm happy too."

What I wanted to be when I was in school: "A nurse. But when I visited a hospital and looked at all the people who were sick, I began to feel ill myself! I knew then there was no way I could handle it."

What a travel agent does

As a travel agent with a large international company, Lois Wong has traveled widely on six continents — North America, Europe, Asia, South America, Africa, and Australia. "I will never forget Africa," she says, recalling her trip to Kruger National Park. "It's vivid in my memory, especially the wildlife. Even the moths were so huge."

Although seeing the world is part of a travel agent's job, the daily reality is something quite different. Lois works with people all day long. "I spend much of my time helping people plan their trips."

Trips to fit a client's needs

Lois listens carefully to her clients to determine their needs. "My clients might be traveling for pleasure, business, or a family emergency. They might just want to book a flight, or they might also need a hotel reservation and a car rental. They might want to go on a 'package' vacation (which includes travel, accommodation, and sight-seeing) or a cruise. Or they might want to travel to several destinations and they need advice on putting their trip together. I check the airline schedules, book the flights, and make the hotel reservations."

In the big suburban mall where her company has one of its many branches, Lois deals mainly with repeat clients (satisfied ones who have used her services before) and referrals (people whose friends or colleagues have recommended her).

Trips for any budget

The finances of Lois' clients vary widely: some have a very strict budget, some are planning a business trip, and some want to splurge on a luxurious holiday. "My job," she says, "is to determine what my clients

World currencies

Can you match these 12 countries with the name of their currency? Answers are on page 48.

Australia	peso
Belgium	krone
Chile	rupee
China	dinar
Denmark	shekel
Germany	dollar
India	yuan
Israel	yen
Italy	ruble
Japan	franc
Kuwait	mark
Russia	lira

need and to book them on the best possible trip."

Most travel agents earn a salary plus a "sliding commission." "I'm paid a small percentage of the cost of the ticket or the package trip," Lois explains. "If I sell many trips in a year, I get a larger percentage. The income can be very good if you work hard."

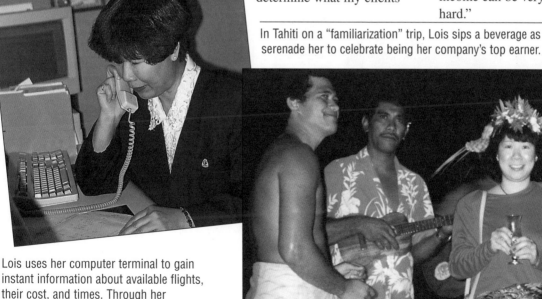

In Tahiti on a "familiarization" trip, Lois sips a beverage as local musicians serenade her to celebrate being her company's top earner.

Lois uses her computer terminal to gain instant information about available flights, their cost, and times. Through her computer, she can book a client on a flight and even write up their ticket.

All in a day's work

Lois's workday is very long, often 10 to 12 hours. "Every morning, I read the papers, watch the news, and keep up on what's happening in the world," she says.

Her job has three main parts — discussions with clients on the phone or at the office, making bookings, and following up with paperwork. "My phone clients are usually 'regulars' — business people who need a flight, hotel, or car," explains Lois. "People who come to my office in person are likely traveling for pleasure. They might also need help with services such as travelers' checks and visas. To visit some countries, you need a visa, issued by that country's government."

"Every time new brochures come in, I must know what's in them. I often read them at home in the bath," she says with a laugh.

What time is it?

When preparing a client's "itinerary," Lois has to keep in mind the world's time zones — or she could reserve a hotel for the wrong day. The itinerary shows the times of departure and arrival. These times depend not only on how long the trip takes but also on how many time zones the traveler crosses. For example, if you leave the eastern part of North America at 10:00 a.m., you may spend five hours flying to the west coast, but arrive at noon because of the change in time zones! Travelers need accurate departure and arrival times especially if they are catching a connecting flight.

How time zones work

In the 19th century, with increasing travel and the invention of the telephone, it became clear that a system of time zones was needed. A system developed by Sir Sandford Fleming, a Canadian, divided the Earth into 24 equal time zones, each 15° of longitude wide and extending from the north to the south poles. (He chose 24 time zones because the Earth takes 24 hours to rotate on its axis.) In 1883, countries around the world agreed to adopt his time zone system. The time zone east of you is one hour ahead of you, while the zone to your west is one hour behind you.

Look at the map. Can you see how many time zones Russia covers? Do you know what time it is in France or Spain when people in Los Angeles or Vancouver are eating breakfast? (The answers are on page 48.)

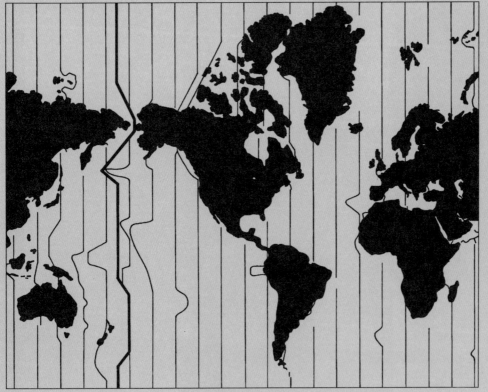

Familiarization trips, called "fam trips" in the business, are hosted by tour operators or airlines. On a recent fam trip, Lois and her son boated on the Amazon River.

Lois has a collection of directories that list almost every hotel in the world, with a brief description and a rating. These directories help her when she needs to book hotels in destinations that she is not familiar with. "I also use my own travel experience when I advise clients," she comments. "I know the best time of year to travel to different places and where to get the best value for your money."

Last minute details

Whether she is booking a simple flight or a trip around the world, Lois pays careful attention to all the details. She asks if clients prefer window or aisle seats, or require a special diet. She also finds out if they have special needs, such as a wheelchair. "I recently booked a flight for a family traveling with three small children and two dogs. They had two stopovers, so I had to make sure they'd have help at all three places." Once she issues a ticket, she tells clients when to be at the airport and any other important details that will make their trip run smoothly.

Don't forget to follow-up

Even after she has booked her clients on trips and issued their tickets and itineraries, Lois's job is not finished. "I make a note to myself to call the clients when they return. I call and ask 'Did you have a good time?,' 'How was your room?,' and so on. By talking to my clients I learn if things have changed since I last went there."

It's a Fact

The global tourist industry is the world's largest employer. In North America and Europe travel for enjoyment is the third largest household expense, after food and housing.

Activity

Plan a trip - in your imagination

You will need
- an atlas or maps
- travel brochures
- an encyclopedia
- optional: access to the Internet

1. Think about where you would like to travel. Pick a theme, such as homes of your ancestors, the upcoming Olympic Games, or the world's highest mountains.
2. Based on your theme, plan to visit three locations in different countries. Find the airport nearest to each place.
3. To prepare for your trip, gather the following information:

- What route will you fly to visit all three places? What airline will you use? Write an itinerary listing the departure and arrival times for each part of your journey.
- What is the time difference between your starting point and each destination?
- What type of money is used in each place?
- What clothes should you take? (Hint: check the climate and weather conditions for each place.)
- How long would you like to spend in each place? What are its main tourist attractions?

How to become a travel agent

Lois grew up in Hong Kong. Even when she was young, she knew she wanted to travel. "Home was such a small piece of island that I always said I wanted to get out and see the world."

She started her career in Hong Kong as a ticket agent. "When I finished high school, I saw an ad in a newspaper that Cathay Pacific Airlines was hiring people. I was very lucky. They picked me as one of five from over 200 applicants, perhaps because I spoke several languages. They trained me so I didn't need any additional schooling." Later, she moved to North America and became a travel agent.

Today, however, it is a good idea to get more education after high

Lois enjoyed a "fam trip" that took her on a luxury cruise up the west coast of North America to Alaska.

school. You can choose from many different travel-related courses. Some colleges offer certificate and degree programs in travel and tourism. In addition, commercial business schools offer travel agent courses. In

many of these, you actually work in a travel agency as part of your education. Most travel agents agree that such on-the-job training is the best education of all.

*I*s this career for you?

To become a travel agent, a sound knowledge of geography is important. "What I don't know, I find out," notes Lois. "I often research information about a destination's climate, hotels, and sights."

It is also important to be very well organized and to pay attention to detail. "Math helps me, too. I often have to compare costs of different types of fares and travel packages in order to get my clients the best value for their money."

Stress is part of the job

You have to stay calm when dealing with people who are rude or upset, and you have to be willing to work long hours. There are always deadlines, constant interruptions, and last-minute changes. "Once I had a big booking, including a cruise, air travel, and hotels — two big trips together," says Lois. "Shortly before departure, the cruise company called me to say they didn't have enough passengers so they had cancelled the cruise. I

"A travel agent must enjoy working with people," Lois advises, "since so much of the day is spent with clients. You need to have good communication skills and be a good listener."

had to plan the whole thing again, at the last minute. Everything else was sold out. Even if you try your best not to make mistakes, things can sometimes get out of control."

Career planning

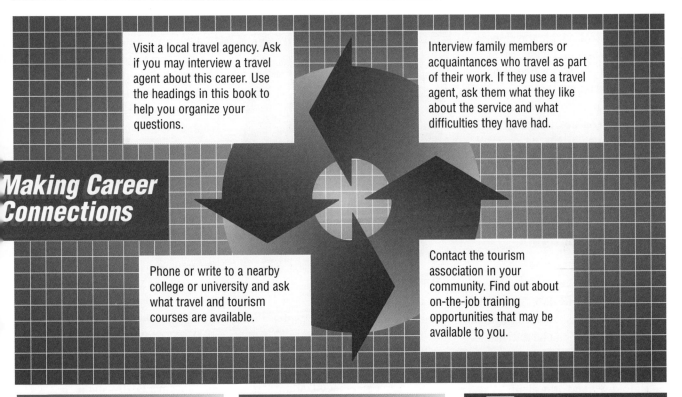

Visit a local travel agency. Ask if you may interview a travel agent about this career. Use the headings in this book to help you organize your questions.

Interview family members or acquaintances who travel as part of their work. If they use a travel agent, ask them what they like about the service and what difficulties they have had.

Making Career Connections

Phone or write to a nearby college or university and ask what travel and tourism courses are available.

Contact the tourism association in your community. Find out about on-the-job training opportunities that may be available to you.

Getting started

Interested in being a travel agent? Here's what you can do now.

1. Keep a travel journal of any family or school trips you go on. This will help you notice and recall details. Your notes may come in handy if you become a travel agent.
2. For an upcoming field trip at school, offer to help make arrangements for transportation, food, and tour guides.
3. Learn a second, third, or even a fourth language. Being able to speak several languages is a real advantage in the travel business.
4. Try to get a part-time or summer sales or service job. Working with people will help improve your communication skills.
5. If you have access to the Internet at school, communicate with "keypals" (like penpals) in countries around the world.
6. In high school, take geography, history, English, math, and computer classes.

Related careers

Here are some related careers you may want to check out.

Information booth attendant
Provides on-the-spot information for travelers looking for lodging, directions, or transportation. May work in malls, bus stations, train stations, or airports.

Tour escort
Accompanies a group of tourists on a package tour. Keeps travelers occupied and happy on long bus rides, solves their problems, and makes sure hotels and restaurants are up to standard. Needs a good sense of humor!

Tour planner
Assembles "package" tours. Organizes transportation and books hotels, sight-seeing tours, and attractions, often for bus-loads of travelers.

Tour-bus guide
Tells tourists about the interesting sights on the tour route. May also drive the bus.

Future watch

In the future, consumers will be able to use their home or office computers to get more of the travel information they need and make their own bookings. Many travel agents may use videos and the Internet to suggest new destinations to their clients. Travel agents will still issue the tickets and, when asked, offer advice about the choices available. In future, it may become even more important for travel agents to have good travel experience to offer their clients.

Harold Zutz — Airline On-Board Service Manager

Every day, all over the world, millions of people travel by airplane. While on board, their needs are looked after by flight attendants. Helping the flight attendants, both in the air and on the ground, are on-board service managers such as Harold Zutz. "We have to meet the airline's standards for safety and service," he comments, "as well as follow strict government regulations on every flight."

Making passengers comfortable

"We want our passengers to have everything they need to make their flight as comfortable and enjoyable as possible. That can be difficult, especially when a plane is carrying 450 people.

Harold worked as a flight attendant for three years so he understands what the job involves. Now he is responsible for more than 200 flight attendants who work on 15 to 20 flights per day. "I coach them, answer their questions, and do whatever I can to make their jobs go more smoothly."

To become a flight attendant, you must have graduated from high school. It helps if you can speak more than one language or have experience working with the public. But, as Harold says, "When an airline hires you, they teach you everything you need to know."

In addition to on-the-job training, he also learned to make effective presentations and to operate a computer. "These skills helped me get the promotion to on-board service manager," smiles Harold.

Trouble-shooting

An on-board service manager examines any flight reports that include unusual happenings. These could be anything from a problem passenger, to difficulties with the meal, to an emergency landing. "If necessary, I try to find out what went wrong," says Harold. "For example, if there were complaints about a

The airline's information systems were recently computerized, which has significantly changed the way it does business. "It is important to be computer-literate in this type of job," Harold says.

"I enjoy being with customers no matter what I'm doing. When I was a flight attendant, my customers were the passengers. Now, my customers are the attendants themselves."

meal, I visit the commissary where the meals are made and investigate."

Once he's assured that a problem won't be repeated, he contacts the person who prepared the report. "It's very important that we respond quickly to complaints. Poor service reflects badly on both the airline and its suppliers."

During the year, an on-board service manager conducts five flight checks. Harold boards early to oversee the safety checks. He observes the flight attendants as they greet passengers, make announcements, distribute refreshments, and handle special requests during the flight. Afterward, he watches as the airplane doors are opened and the passengers get off. "Flight checks are designed to monitor the quality of service that the airline provides and see where we can improve it," Harold explains. "We're not there to spy but to help the attendants do their jobs better."

Getting started

1. Try to get a part-time job working with people.
2. Take safety training, such as lifeguarding or cardiopulmonary resuscitation (CPR).
3. Learn as many languages as you can.
4. If you are taking a flight, ask if you can interview a flight attendant during a quiet time.

Helen Huggett — Safari Planner

Helen Huggett is building an unusual business — taking small groups on safari, to see the breathtaking landscapes and wildlife in the game parks of Kenya.

A keen naturalist (someone who studies plants and animals), Helen worked as a volunteer tour guide at a zoo for several years. One year, she joined a zookeepers' safari to Kenya. When she returned home, she decided to start a safari business so she could keep returning to East Africa.

Making travel arrangements

Once Helen decides where her next trip will be, she and her partner in Kenya, Ahmed Akbar, make the arrangements. They find out the costs for food, transportation, and accommodation from the time the tourists land in Kenya's capital, Nairobi.

"Then, I advertise in about six different magazines for naturalists, animal lovers, and bird watchers. I do this about a year before the trip."

The Kenyan boys beside Helen follow the traditional Samburu male custom: they dye their hair red with ocher — a natural pigment from iron-rich earth.

"On our last trip, we stopped the van to watch baboons," says Helen. "A big male approached us. All of a sudden he made a lunge through the van window — toward a papaya that was sitting on the dashboard. The quick-thinking driver tossed the papaya out of the van. The baboon grabbed it and ran away."

"The bonus of tenting is that you experience all the smells and hear the night animal sounds," says Helen. "It's just marvellous."

Just how rough is it?

When you're traveling in Kenya, it takes a long time to get from one place to another because the roads are rough. "Our group of 10 visitors travels in two minivans. Everyone has a window seat," says Helen.

In the game parks, the visitors see gazelles, giraffes, elephants, rhinoceroses, hyenas, lions, and apes. They visit different habitats — mountains, savannah (grassland), riverine forest (along the river's edge), and ocean coast. That way, they see many different animals.

When driving through the game parks, Helen tries not to disturb the plants and animals. "I don't think it's fair to the animals to crowd around and destroy their hunt. Also, our schedule is loose, so if we want to stop and watch a herd of elephants for an hour, we do it."

Visitors stay in luxury tents that are all set up. "They're like a regular hotel with canvas walls," Helen says. "And the food is excellent."

Getting started

1. Read about animals or parts of the world that you find particularly interesting.
2. If you have access to the Internet, join a naturalists' newsgroup.
3. Watch television nature programs.
4. In high school, take science and geography courses. Business courses would also help.

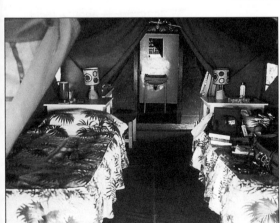

Catherine George — Travel Writer

See the world — and get paid for it! That's the allure for travel writer and editor, Catherine George.

Catherine works for a large daily newspaper. In addition to writing a regular travel column, she puts together the newspaper's large weekly travel section. She decides which themes and subjects the section will cover each week. Then she chooses topics, assigns and edits articles, supervises page layout, and writes headlines. With members of the newspaper's art department, she also selects photos and illustrations for the articles.

"Putting out a travel section takes time, research, and organization," Catherine explains. "We start assigning articles to the writers almost a year before they'll appear in the paper."

Keeping up with trends

"The search for new ideas is a challenge," she adds. "In order to stay on top of developing trends, I regularly read the travel sections of other major newspapers. I also attend promotions put on by tourist boards, resorts, hotels, and travel agents."

"Keep it as simple as possible and don't use too many glowing adjectives or big words," advises Catherine on travel writing. "People want to know the basics — how to get there, where to stay, what to see, and what it will cost."

Certain themes come up regularly — skiing vacations and Caribbean travel are common during winter, for instance. But as much as possible, the newspaper tries to come up with new angles and trends. "For example," notes Catherine, "recent political changes in Eastern Europe have made that area an increasingly popular destination."

Many travel writers are graduates of journalism schools, but Catherine took a different route to this career. Early in her working life, she conducted title searches for real estate transactions. From there, she moved to the newspaper business as a researcher, checking the facts in travel articles.

"When I started out, I didn't know much about writing. I didn't even know what a 'lead' was," she recalls. "I soon learned — it's the introductory paragraph in an article. My editor encouraged me to try writing and I worked my way up. If you want to write, just do it. Writing is a skill you can learn. The more you do it, the better you get."

Traveling

While she enjoys her job, Catherine says that it's not always as glamorous as it seems. She has traveled so much over the years that she now prefers to spend her vacations at home.

"My ancestors moved away from this stone house in Ireland in the 1850s," says Catherine. "I found it while on assignment in Ireland."

Getting started

1. Write an article about a recent trip you took. Illustrate the story with photographs and maps.
2. Work on your school newspaper or yearbook doing writing, editing, layout, and photography.
3. Read the travel sections of newspapers and magazines to see how professionals handle their subject matter.
4. Take courses in language arts and geography.

Bob Khasnabish — Travel Entrepreneur

Bob Khasnabish and his brother Richard own a travel company that specializes in holidays to faraway places. Unusual trips are the norm for the Khasnabish brothers, who were born in Burma. "When I was 15," Bob recalls, "I left Burma to join my brother, Richard, who had already moved to North America." With travel "in his blood," Bob chose his career easily. He took a one-year business administration course and a three-year course in travel and tourism. After graduation, he and Richard set up Wings of the World, Inc.

Being there first

Bob makes about five trips a year. He travels for about three months in Central and South America, Africa, and Asia. There he meets with government officials, tourist board employees, hotel and sightseeing tour operators, and airline managers. "I like being the first to see the tourist possibilities of remote spots," says Bob.

The first group

Once Bob has completed the arrangements for a new trip, he becomes the tour leader for the first group. As tour leader, he supervises everything, from the quality of the breakfast to the air conditioning on the bus, to make sure the travelers are content.

Only two populations of giant tortoises have survived in the world: one on Aldabra, a tiny island in the Indian Ocean, and the other on the Galapagos Islands in the Pacific Ocean. These creatures weigh as much as 250 kg (600 pounds) and live up to 200 years. The tortoises have been threatened by, among others, goats brought to the Galapagos by 19th-century explorers. The goats trampled and ate tortoise eggs to the point where the population almost died out. Now, with goat control, the tortoises are surviving.

The Galapagos Islands are just one of many exotic places where Bob takes tours every year.

Impact of tourists

Bob knows that tourism brings both benefits and drawbacks to remote countries. "It brings in tourist dollars and creates jobs for the residents," he notes, "but it can also change people's ways of life forever. We also have to be careful not to damage wildlife."

Take the Galapagos, for instance. The Galapagos Islands are a popular tourist destination. This string of small volcanic islands, located in the Pacific Ocean off the coast of Ecuador, is home to plants and animals found nowhere else in the world. To protect the wildlife, only a few tourists may visit at one time, and they aren't allowed to stay on the island overnight. During the day, they walk only on the islands' paths, viewing strange and fascinating tortoises, birds, and plant life. With this protection, the tourists can visit without the risk of destroying the very place they want to see.

Exciting trips

Among the exciting trips Wings of the World offers are Antarctica by ship and an elegant railway trip by steam locomotive through Tanzania, Zambia, Zimbabwe, and South Africa with a railway historian. Another trip visits Preah Vihear, a spectacular temple perched on the edge of a sheer, cliff precipice in the mountains of Cambodia.

Getting started

1. Read travel magazines and the travel sections of newspapers. Find out what types of trips are most popular.
2. Plan a day of sight-seeing for a visitor to your community. Collect brochures, maps, articles, and postcards to help you prepare an itinerary.
3. In high school, take geography, science, and business courses.

Classified Advertising

Help Wanted

PLASTERER/CARPENTER/ PAINTER required for historical renovations. Min 5 yr experience. References required. Send resumé to Joe's Times, 982 Knab St., Arundel, Province/ State, Postal/Zip Code

COURT REPORTER FOR LAW COURTS IN REMOTE AREA. Qualified and certified reporter with some exams. All office support provided. Good salary and transcript fees. Call Joe Shymanski at Northern Employment Services Ltd., 555-1030

Sci-Connections

Sci-Connections is a world leader in providing top-of-the-line equipment to the cable television and te... industries. We currently have the foll...ing opportunities:

DESIGN ENGINEER
Ideal candidate will have a BSEE...d 5-10 years experience w... tal telephony, DATACOM, ...XX Micro Processor... FPGA. Experience with A... or similar de... capture tools and solid... C and Assembly... gramming l... guages is pr... ferred.

TELEPHONY ... INTERFACE ...S. ENGINEER
Position re...es E... (MSEE pr...ed) ... 7+ years ...erience ... analog and ...ital des... related to ...ctronic ... telephony ...e inte... application... ... ETSI/ANSI ...ecifica... Microproces... d... experience al... equired...

SOFTWARE ...
Ideal cand...

FLIGHT ATTEND...
experienced, for a large established company's private corporate jet. Totally bilingual in Spanish & English, also Chinese & Russian an asset. Fax resumé to 555-4618

PLASTERS/ACRYLIC FINISHERS —

Experienced only need apply. Call 555-7800, ask for Ross.

SAUSAGE
maker req'd. immed. Must have diploma in food services & min. 3 yrs. exp. 555-7358.

...mmunicati...
is a lead...

METAL FABRICATOR
for rust repair/customizing ...otor vehicles. Must be skilled ...making auto panels. Own to... req. Fax resumé: 555-23...

CRU...E SHIP JOBS!
Year ro... positions. Hiring ...th men...omen. Free room & ...ard. Wi...ain. Call, 24 hrs, ...5-7778.

...AN 80 b... seniors home ...requir... Food Service ...uperv...r/Chef live-in. ...ven...t country living. ...re...mé to 555-5564..

...established restaurant ...ng creative kitchen ...nnel, 2 positions avail- ...ef De Partie & Jr Sous ...Send resumés to 34 ...Street, Gardenia City, Province/State, Postal/Zip Code

...ourier Servi...es Unlimited
...r Paralegal/Law Cl...
You will pro...ory assistance to corporate lawyers handling a variety of legal matters including diverse projects, the day-to-day flow of documents and information, and the development and administration of control systems and procedures.

The successful candidate will have a bachelor's degree/equivalent. Paralegal/Law Clerk training and Certificate required. Must have a minimum of four (4) years of Paralegal/Law Clerk work experience. Excellent research and writing skills as well as strong organizational, human relations and communication skills are required.

We offer our employees an excellent starting salary and an exceptional benefits plan which includes vision/dental/medical coverage, and a generous pension plan. Please send your resumé in confidence to:

CSU, Personnel Department, 4390 Parkwood East, Suite 392, Missangi, Province/State, Postal/Zip Code.

Willow Island Tourist Bureau

The Willow Island Tourist Bureau needs an additional staff member for July and August to help visitors find accommodation and to answer questions about local restaurants, sports facilities, and events. Applicants must be available to work evenings and weekends as well as daytime. The successful candidate speaks English clearly, has a pleasant manner, and has some computer experience. Ability to speak a second language is an asset. Please apply in writing to:

Susan Lee, Manager
Willow Island Tourist Bureau
Province/State
Postal/Zip Code

Who got the job?

Finding a job

- Talk with family, friends, and neighbors, and let them know what jobs interest you.
- Respond to "Help Wanted" ads in newspapers.

- Post an advertisement of your skills on a community bulletin board.

- Send out inquiry letters to companies and follow up with phone calls.

A job application usually consists of a letter and a resumé (a summary of your experience, including volunteer work, as well as your qualifications for the job). Applicants whose resumés show they are qualified may be invited to a job interview.

- Register at government employment offices and private employment agencies.
- Contact potential employers by phone or in person.

Activity

Getting a summer job

The advertisement shown on the opposite page, for a summer staff member at the Willow Island Tourist Bureau, was placed in a local newspaper. Richard Mak and Theresa Goncalves are two of the applicants Susan Lee wants to consider for the job. Their letters and resumés, and the notes made by Susan Lee during the interviews, are shown on pages 46 and 47.

Procedure

Make a list of the qualifications you think Susan Lee will take into consideration in deciding whom to hire. Then list the strengths and weaknesses in each applicant's resumé, covering letter, and performance during the interview. Which person would you hire? Why?

Challenge

If you were being interviewed for this job, how would you perform? Begin by describing your skills and experience to the interviewer. It is also a good idea to prepare questions to help you find out what the job actually requires and to show the interviewer you have a genuine interest in this kind of work. Practice by role-playing a job interview with a friend. Take turns playing the interviewer and the applicant. Role-playing gives you practice asking and answering questions comfortably, so that when you go for an interview, you'll have a better chance of getting the job.

Richard Mak's application and interview

43 Abbot Trail
Merrickville, Province/State
Postal/Zip Code
555-1741

April 26, 19—

Ms. Susan Lee
Manager
Willow Island Tourist Bureau
Province/State
Postal/Zip Code

Dear Ms. Lee:

I read your recent ad for a staff member for July and August.

I am a recent graduate of Merrickville High School and plan to enroll in the hospitality program at Huron College in September.

As my resumé shows, I have considerable experience working with the public. I am familiar with word processing software and speak Cantonese as well as English. As well, I enjoy a variety of outdoor sports, including tennis, swimming, and water skiing.

I would appreciate an interview. Thank you for your consideration.

Sincerely,

Richard Mak

Richard Mak

Interview: Richard Mak

- arrived early
- dressed in a polo shirt and casual pants
- personable, lots of self-confidence, expresses himself well
- asked good questions about the job
- admitted to being slow at inputting, but is good with our new point-and-click system.
- enjoys working with the public, feels this would be good experience
- hopes to work in tourism industry

Richard D. Mak
43 Abbot Trail
Merrickville, Province/State
Postal/Zip Code

Education
19— - 19—

Merrickville High School, Gradua with honors.
I took geography, history and Engl courses this past year, and w associate editor of the scho yearbook. I was a member of the sw team throughout high school.

Employment
Summer 19—

Merrickville Parks and Recreation Dep In my work as a public relation assistant, I responded to publi inquiries, conducted tours of recreatio facilities, and answered telephone calls.

Winter 19—

J.E.K. Enterprises, Merrickville
As a part-time sales assistant, I dealt with customer inquiries and handled cash receipts. I had a thorough knowledge of the products I sold.

References Available on request

Theresa Goncalves' application and interview

830 Augusta St.
Oxford Landing, Province/State
Postal/Zip Code

April 28, 19—

Ms. Susan Lee
Manager
Willow Island Tourist Bureau
Province/State
Postal/Zip Code

Dear Ms. Lee:

I am very interested in the position of staff member at the Willow Island Tourist Bureau this summer.

I enjoy working with the public and hope to have a career in the public relations field after I graduate from college. My previous jobs have given me considerable experience in working with customers and meeting their needs. I am experienced in using computers and have helped other students learn to use them. I am fluent in French and Spanish.

Please call me at 555-3821 in order to arrange an interview. I look forward to hearing from you.

Sincerely

Theresa Goncalves

Theresa M. Goncalves

Interview: Theresa Goncalves

- arrived on time, dressed in slacks and a sweater.
- likes working with people and gets a feeling of accomplishment from helping them find what they're looking for
- was very comfortable talking about using computers at school
- intelligent, speaks directly but very softly
- wants a summer job as she is saving to go to college

Resumé

Theresa M. Goncalves
830 Augusta St.
Oxford Landing, Province/State
Postal/Zip Code

Education

Completed high school at Merrickville High School (French immersion program)
- volunteer teacher's aid at local French-language school
- volunteered at the community food bank
- school volleyball team member

Work Experience

Summer 19— Puffin Gear, Oxford Landing, Sales Representative
- made sales
- placed orders
- handled customer inquiries

Summer 19— Merrickville Community Day Care, Child care assistant
- looked after a group of preschool children
- handled inquiries from parents and others

Winter 19— Oxford Landing Animal Clinic, Receptionist/secretary (part-time)
- handled telephone inquiries and got information from pet owners
- developed good typing and computer skills

References On request

Index

accommodation, 35
accounting, 24
administration, 32
advertise, 41
agenda, 17, 19
airline manager, 43
airline on-board service
 manager, 40
audiovisual person, 18

back-of-the-house, 29
bellhop, 29, 31
boating regulations, 27
booking, 19, 20, 33, 35
bookkeeping, 24
brochures, 43
budget, 17, 21, 24
business administration
 course, 33, 43, 41

cancellation, 19, 20
car rental, 35
cardiopulmonary
 resuscitation (CPR),
 27, 40
caterer, 17-19, 21
chairperson, 19
chef, 9
climate, 37, 38
commissary, 40
communication skills, 15,
 38
communications course,
 33
community events, 15
computer class, 39
conference, 16, 30
cruise, 35
curator, 15

deadline, 38
design class, 21
door and front desk staff,
 29

editor, 42
engineering, 29
environmental
 regulations, 27
event host, 18
excursion, 24

familiarization trip, 35,
 37
festival organizer, 4-9
field trip, 39
flight attendant, 40
food and beverage
 manager, 30
front-desk manager, 18,
 30

game park, 41
geography, 38, 39, 41-43
government regulations,
 40
guest services manager,
 28-33

historic site, 11
historic site administrator,
 15
historical interpreter, 10-
 15
historical researcher, 15
history, 39
hospitality industry, 20
hotel manager, 21, 30
hotel management
 program, 20, 33
hotel's sales director, 18

housekeeping services
 manager, 20, 30
human resources
 manager, 30

information specialist,
 15
interactive videodiscs, 33
itinerary, 36, 37, 43

language skills, 31, 33,
 39, 40, 42

marina operators, 22-27
math, 39
meeting and convention
 planner, 16-21
museum guide, 15

organizational skills, 20,
 21, 32
orienteering group, 27

paperwork, 24
peak season, 23
planning session, 30
presentations, 14
promotion, 32, 42
public relations organizer,
 9

recreation director, 21
rental services provider,
 21
researcher, 42

safari planner, 41
schedule, 29
science, 43
sights, 38
sliding commission, 35
special diet, 36

telecommunications, 21
ticket agent, 38
tour guide, 21, 37, 39, 43
tourist attraction, 37
tourist board employee,
 43
trainee, 31, 33
travel journal, 39
travel and tourism
 program, 38, 43
travel entrepreneur, 43
travel agent, 34-39
travel writer, 42
travelers' check, 36

video conference, 21
visa, 36
volunteer, 21

wildlife, 35, 43
world currencies, 35

Answers

Answers to currency quiz on page 35

Country	Currency
Australia	dollar
Belgium	franc
Chile	peso
China	yuan
Denmark	krone
Germany	mark
India	rupee
Israel	shekel
Italy	lira
Japan	yen
Kuwait	dinar
Russia	ruble

Answers to time zone questions on page 36:
Russia covers 11 time zones.

It's 4 p.m. in Western Europe when people on the west coast of North America are having breakfast at 8 a.m.

Credits

(l = left; r = right; t = top; b = bottom; c = center; bl = bottom left; br = bottom right)

All illustrations by Warren Clark.

All photographs by Jo Anne Sommers, except 5, 6, 8 Robert D. Watkins; 11 (t), 12 (r), 13 (t) (b), 14 (t) Fort York; 20, 25 Canadian Tourism Commission; 29 Four Seasons Washington; 35 (r), 37, 38 (t) Lois Wong: 41 Helen Huggett; 42 (b) Catherine George; 43 Wings of the World.